EVERYMAN

& The Second Shepherd's Play

Anonymous

PRESTWICK HOUSE
LITERARY TOUCHSTONE CLASSICS™

P.O. Box 658 • Clayton, Delaware 19938

Senior Editor: Paul Moliken

Editors: Darlene Gilmore and Sondra Y. Abel

Cover Design: Maria J. Mendoza

Production: Jerry Clark

Prestwick House
Literary Touchstone Classics

P.O. Box 658 • Clayton, Delaware 19938
Tel: 1.800.932.4593
Fax: 1.888.718.9333
Web: www.prestwickhouse.com

Prestwick House Teaching Units™, Activity Packs™, and Response Journals™ are the perfect complement for these editions. To purchase teaching resources for this book, visit www.prestwickhouse.com/material

This Prestwick House edition is an unabridged republication with slight emendations of *Everyman* and *The Second Shepherds' Play* published in 1910 by Houghton Mifflin Co., New York.

ISBN 978-1-58049-850-0

EVERYMAN

& The Second Shepherd's Play

CONTENTS

NOTES

What is a literary classic and why are these classic works important to the world?

A literary classic is a work of the highest excellence that has something important to say about life and/or the human condition and says it with great artistry. A classic, through its enduring presence, has withstood the test of time and is not bound by time, place, or customs. It speaks to us today as forcefully as it spoke to people one hundred or more years ago, and as forcefully as it will speak to people of future generations. For this reason, a classic is said to have universality.

The use of plays to educate the16th century English audience on virtues, the predominance of archetypes and flat characters, and the simplicity of plot are staples of the genres known as Cycle and Morality Plays. Most members of a typical audience of the time could barely read or write, and the teachings of the Church were predominantly in Latin; therefore, the theater was a seemingly perfect way to reach and instruct the population. The drama evolved from the Bible, so the stories were familiar and could be capitalized upon; the plays were, therefore, sanctioned by the religious authorities, which had in the past and would in the future, condemn actors and acting. Traveling "tropes" of players would set up a stage in a small town and perform for the residents. Frequently, members of trade guilds also were part of the cast.

While the characters in *Everyman* and *The Second Shepherds' Play* are one-dimensional, they do provide the impetus for some later Elizabethan drama (Marlowe's *Faust*, for example), and these two are considered the epitome of this type. However, audiences soon lost interest in the simplistic drama being presented and demanded more realistic, elaborate, and compelling theater, which set the stage for the rise of Elizabethan drama.

EVERYMAN

Reading Pointers for Sharper Insights

Everyman is one of the last and most well known plays of the 15th century genre called Morality Plays. The author of *Everyman* is unknown, but the play is believed to be the English translation of an earlier Dutch version, *Elckerlyc*, written in 1495. Although it's unclear exactly when *Everyman* was written, the last early editions of the play were printed between 1521 and 1537. The following information will assist you in understanding *Everyman* and the role it played in medieval society:

- Morality Plays were developed as allegorical presentations of the conflict between virtue and vice. Most of the people during this time were illiterate, and morality plays were used to instruct people in a manner they could identify with.
- These plays were often parables (i.e., stories that teach a lesson). The lesson for Everyman, the character, is that death is inevitable, so one must prepare for God's judgment by leading a virtuous life.
- The Catholic Church was an integral part of medieval society. People led their lives based on the doctrines of the Church, as presented by priests, who frequently used stories to teach biblical precepts.
- In addition to morality, religious ideology was the focus of many plays, including these two.

Characters:

In contrast to modern plays that use multi-dimensional characters who have individual qualities, *Everyman*, as is typical of most Morality Plays, employs one-dimensional characters to represent people, things, events, or symbols. For example, some characters in the play stand for specific traits, occurrences, or people:

- Everyman – the common individual; the ordinary church attendee
- Fellowship – friends, acquaintances, colleagues
- Goods – material possessions, wealth
- Good Deeds – virtues
- Knowledge – intellect

Themes:

Several closely related themes are presented in *Everyman*, which are represented by the words and actions of the characters. As you read *Everyman*, the following concepts should become apparent:

- Giving to others is more rewarding than acquiring wealth and possessions.
- People are responsible for their own actions.
- The only thing humans can take with them in death is the virtue they lived with during life.
- Overindulgence leads to sin.
- God will forgive those who repent.
- Virtuous living is the path to salvation.

EVERYMAN

NOTE

The opinion has been commonly accepted that the English version of the play was a translation from the Dutch version *Elckerlyc* ascribed to Dorlandus. The chief support of this view is the fact that the Dutch version was printed before the English. It may be safer to consider the question still open, for either may be the earlier, and both may go back to an earlier version, now lost.

Here beginneth a treatise how the High Father of Heaven sendeth Death to summon every creature to come and give an account of their lives in this world, and is in manner of a moral play.

[*The Messenger enters.*

Messenger.
 I pray you all give your audience,
 And hear this matter with reverence,
  In form a moral play.
 The Summoning of Everyman it is called so,
 That of our lives and ending maketh show   5
  How transitory we be every day.
 This matter is wondrous precious,
 But the meaning of it is more gracious
  And sweet to bear away.
 The story saith: Man, in the beginning   10

Watch well, and take good heed of the ending,
    Be you never so gay!
Ye think sin in the beginning full sweet,
Which, in the end, causeth the soul to weep,
    When the body lieth in clay.   15
Here shall you see how Fellowship and Jollity,
Both Strength, Pleasure, and Beauty,
    Will fade from thee as flower in May,
For ye shall hear how our Heaven's King
Calleth Everyman to a general reckoning.   20
    Give audience and hear what he doth say.
                               [The Messenger goes.

God speaketh:
I perceive, here in my majesty,
    How that all creatures be to me unkind,
Living, without fear, in worldly prosperity.
    In spiritual vision the people be so blind,   25
Drowned in sin, they know me not for their God;
    In worldly riches is all their mind.
They fear not my righteousness, the sharp rod.
    My law that I disclosed, when I for them died,
They clean forget, and shedding of my blood red.   30
    I hung between two it cannot be denied,
To get them life I suffered to be dead,
I healed their feet, with thorns was hurt my head.
    I could do no more than I did truly,
And now I see the people do clean forsake me;   35
They use the seven deadly sins† damnable
    In such wise that pride, covetousness, wrath, and lechery,
Now in this world be made commendable,
    And thus they leave of angels the heavenly company.
Every man liveth so after his own pleasure,   40
And yet of their lives they be nothing sure.
The more I them forbear, I see
The worse from year to year they be;
All that live grow more evil apace;
Therefore I will, in briefest space,†   45
From every man in person have a reckoning shown.
For, if I leave the people thus alone
In their way of life and wicked passions to be,†
They will become much worse than beasts, verily.
Now for envy would one eat up another, and tarry not   50

---

†Terms marked in the text with (†) can be looked up in the Glossary for additional information.

Charity is by all clean forgot.
I hoped well that every man
In my glory should make his mansion,
And thereto I made them all elect,
But now I see, like traitors abject, 55
They thank me not for the pleasure that I for them meant,
Nor yet for their being that I them have lent.
I proffered the people great multitude of mercy,
And few there be that ask it heartily.
They be so cumbered with worldly riches, thereto 60
I must needs upon them justice do,—
On every man living without fear.
Where art thou, Death, thou mighty messenger?

[*Death enters.*

Death.
Almighty God, I am here at your will,
Your commandment to fulfil. 65

God.
Go thou to Everyman,
And show him in my name
A pilgrimage he must on him take,
Which he in no wise may escape,
And that he bring with him a sure reckoning 70
Without delay or any tarrying.

Death.
Lord, I will in the world go run over all,
And cruelly search out both great and small.
Every man will I beset that liveth beastly
Out of God's law, and doth not dread folly. 75
He that loveth riches I will strike with my dart
His sight to blind and him from heaven to part—
Except if Alms be his good friend—
In hell for to dwell, world without end.
Lo, yonder I see Everyman walking. 80
Full little he thinketh on my coming!
His mind is on fleshly lusts and his treasure,
And great pain it shall cause him to endure
Before the Lord, of Heaven the King.
Everyman, stand still! Whither art thou going 85
Thus gayly? Hast thou thy Maker forgot?

[*Everyman enters.*

Everyman.
Why askest thou?
Wouldest thou know? For what?

Death.
Yea, sir, I will show you now.
In great haste I am sent to thee					90
From God, out of his majesty.

Everyman.
What, sent to me!

Death.
Yea, certainly.
Though thou hast forgot him here,
He thinketh on thee in the heavenly sphere,					95
As, ere we part, thou shalt know.

Everyman.
What desireth God of me?

Death.
That shall I show thee.
A reckoning he will needs have
	Without any longer respite.					100

Everyman.
To give a reckoning longer leisure I crave.
	This blind matter troubleth my wit.

Death.
Upon thee thou must take a long journey,
	Therefore, do thou thine accounting-book with thee bring.
For turn again thou canst not by no way,					105
	And look thou be sure in thy reckoning,
For before God thou shalt answer, and show true
Thy many bad deeds and good but a few,
How thou hast spent thy life and in what wise
Before the Chief Lord of Paradise.					110
Get thee prepared that we may be upon that journey,
For well thou knowest thou shalt make none for thee attorney.†

Everyman.
Full unready I am such reckoning to give.
I know thee not. What messenger art thou?

Death.

I am Death that no man fear, 115
For every man I arrest and no man spare,
For it is God's commandment
That all to me should be obedient.

Everyman.

O Death, thou comest when I had thee least in mind!
In thy power it lieth to save me yet ;—
Thereto of my goods will I give thee, if thou wilt be kind,— 120
Yea, a thousand pounds shalt thou get!—
And defer this matter till another day.

Death.

Everyman, it may not be in any way.
I set no store by gold, silver, riches, or such gear, 125
Nor by pope, emperor, king, prince, or peer.†
For, if I would receive gifts great,
All the world I might get,
But my custom is clean the contrary way.
I give thee no respite. Come hence, nor delay! 130

Everyman.

Alas, shall I have no longer respite!
I may say Death giveth no warning!
To think on thee, it maketh my heart sick,
For all unready is my book of reckoning.
But if I might have twelve years of waiting, 135
My accounting-book I would make so clear
That my reckoning I should not need to fear.
Wherefore, Death, I pray thee, for God's mercy,
Spare me till I be provided with a remedy!

Death.

It availeth thee not to cry, weep, and pray, 140
But haste thee lightly, that thou mayest be on thy journey,
And make proof of thy friends, if thou can,
For, know thou well, time waiteth for no man,
And in the world each living creature
Because of Adam's sin† must die by nature. 145

Everyman.

Death, if I should this pilgrimage take,
And my reckoning duly make,
Show me, for Saint Charity,†
Should I not come again shortly?

Death.
No, Everyman, if once thou art there,   150
Thou mayest nevermore come here,
Trust me, verily.

Everyman.
O gracious God, in the high seat celestial,
    Have mercy on me in this utmost need!
Shall I no company have from this vale terrestrial[†]   155
    Of mine acquaintance that way me to lead?

Death.
Yea, if any be so hardy
As to go with thee and bear thee company.
Haste thee that thou mayest be gone to God's magnificence,
Thy reckoning to give before his presence.   160
What, thinkest thou thy life is given thee,
    And thy worldly goods also?

Everyman.
I had thought so, verily.

Death.
Nay, nay, it was but lent to thee,
For, as soon as thou dost go,   165
Another a while shall have it and then even so,
    Go therefore as thou hast done.
Everyman, thou art mad! Thou hast thy wits five,[†]
And here on earth will not amend thy life,
    For suddenly I do come!   170

Everyman.
O wretched caitiff, whither shall I flee
    That I may escape this endless sorrow!
    Nay, gentle Death, spare me until to-morrow
That I may amend me
With good avisement!   175

Death.
Nay, thereto I will not consent,
Nor no man respite, if I might,
But to the heart suddenly I shall smite
Without any "advisement."
And now out of thy sight I will me hie,   180
See that thou make thee ready speedily,

For thou mayest say this is the day
Wherefrom no man living may escape away.

Everyman.
Alas, I may well weep with sighs deep!
    Now have I no manner of company   185
To help me on my journey and me to keep,
    And also my writing is all unready.
What can I do that may excuse me!
    I would to God I had never been begot!
To my soul a full great profit it would be,[†]   190
    For now I fear pains huge and great, God wot!
The time passeth—help, Lord, that all things wrought!
For, though I mourn, yet it availeth naught.
The day passeth and is almost through,
I wot not well of aught that I may do.   195
To whom were it best that I my plaint should make?
What if to Fellowship I thereof spake,
And what this sudden chance should mean disclosed?
For surely in him is all my trust reposed—
We have in the world so many a day   200
Been good friends in sport and play.
I see him yonder certainly—
I trust that he will bear me company;
Therefore to him will I speak to ease my sorrow.
Well met, good Fellowship, and a good morrow!   205
                [*Enter* **Fellowship.**

Fellowship speaketh:
    I wish thee good morrow, Everyman, by this day![†]
        Sir, why lookest thou so piteously?
    If anything be amiss, prithee to me it say
        That I may help in remedy.

Everyman.
Yea, good Fellowship, yea,   210
    I am in great jeopardy!

Fellowship.
My true friend, show to me your mind.
I will not forsake thee to my live's end,
In the way of good company.

Everyman.
That was well spoken and lovingly.   215

Fellowship.
Sir, I must needs know your heaviness.
I have pity to see you in any distress.
If any have wronged you, revenged ye shall be,
Though I upon the ground be slain for thee,
Even should I know before that I should die.   220

Everyman.
Verily, Fellowship, gramercy!†

Fellowship.
Tush! By thy thanks I set not a straw.
Show me your grief and say no more.

Everyman.
If I my heart should to you unfold,
        And you then were to turn your heart from me,   225
And no comfort would give when I had told,
        Then should I ten times sorrier be.

Fellowship.
Sir, I say as I will do indeed!

Everyman.
Then you be a good friend at need.
I have found you true heretofore.   230

Fellowship.
And so ye shall evermore,
For, in faith, if thou goest to hell,
        I will not forsake thee by the way.

Everyman.
Ye speak like a good friend—I believe you well.
        I shall deserve it, if so I may!   235

Fellowship.
I speak of no deserving, by this day,
For he that will say, and nothing do,
Is not worthy with good company to go.
Therefore show me the grief of your mind,
As to your friend most loving and kind.   240

Everyman.
I shall show you how it is:
        Commanded I am to go a journey,

A long way hard and dangerous,
  And give a strict account without delay
  Before the High Judge, Adonai.†   245
Wherefore, I pray you, bear me company,
As ye have promised, on this journey.

Fellowship.
That is matter, indeed! Promise is duty—
But if I should take such a voyage on me,
I know well it should be to my pain;   250
Afeard also it maketh me, for certain.
But let us take counsel here as well as we can,
For your words would dismay a strong man.

Everyman.
Why, if I had need, ye said
Ye would never forsake me, quick nor dead,   255
Though it were to hell truly!

Fellowship.
So I said certainly,
But such pleasant things be set aside, the truth to say;
And also, if we took such a journey,
When should we come again?   260

Everyman.
Nay, never again till the day of doom.

Fellowship.
In faith, then, will I not come there.
  Who hath you these tidings brought?

Everyman.
Indeed, Death was with me here.

Fellowship.
  Now, by God that all hath bought,   265
If Death were the messenger,
For no man living here below
I will not that loathly journey go—
Not for the father that begat me!

Everyman.
Ye promised otherwise, pardy!†   270

Fellowship.
I know well I do say so, truly,
  And still, if thou wilt eat and drink and make good cheer,
Or haunt of women the merry company,
  I would not forsake you while the day is clear,
Trust me, verily.   275

Everyman.
Yea, thereto ye would be ready!
  To go to mirth, solace, and play,
Your mind would sooner persuaded be
  Than to bear me company on my long journey.

Fellowship.
Now, in good sooth, I have no will that way—   280
But if thou would'st murder, or any man kill,
In that I will help thee with a good will.

Everyman.
Oh, that is simple advice, indeed!
  Gentle Fellowship, help me in my necessity!
We have loved long, and now I am in need!   285
  And now, gentle Fellowship, remember me!

Fellowship.
Whether ye have loved me or no,
By Saint John, I will not with thee go!

Everyman.
Yea, I pray thee, take this task on thee and do so much for me,
As to bring me forward on my way for Saint Charity, 290
And comfort me till I come without the town.

Fellowship.
Nay, if thou wouldest give me a new gown,
I will not a foot with thee go.
But, if thou hadst tarried, I would not have left thee so.
And so now, God speed thee on thy journey,   295
For from thee I will depart as fast as I may!

Everyman.
Whither away, Fellowship? Will you forsake me?

Fellowship.
Yea, by my faith! I pray God take thee.

Everyman.
Farewell, good Fellowship,—for thee my heart is sore.
Adieu forever, I shall see thee no more! 300

Fellowship.
In faith, Everyman, farewell now at the ending.
For you I will remember that parting is grieving.
                              [*Fellowship goes.*

Everyman.
Alack! Shall we thus part indeed?
        Ah, Lady, help! Lo, vouchsafing no more comfort,
Fellowship thus forsaketh me in my utmost need. 305
        For help in this world whither shall I resort?
Fellowship heretofore with me would merry make,
And now little heed of my sorrow doth he take.
It is said in prosperity men friends may find
Which in adversity be full unkind. 310
Now whither for succor shall I flee,
Since that Fellowship hath forsaken me?
To my kinsmen will I truly,
Praying them to help me in my necessity.
I believe that they will do so 315
For "Nature will creep where it may not go."†
                        [*Kindred and Cousin*† *enter.*
I will go try, for yonder I see them go.
Where be ye now, my friends and kinsmen, lo?

Kindred.
Here we be now at your commandment.
Cousin, I pray you show us your intent 320
In any wise and do not spare.

Cousin.
Yea, Everyman, and to us declare
If ye be disposed to go any whither,
For, wit you well, we will live and die together!

Kindred.
In wealth and woe we will with you hold,
For "with his own kin a man may be bold." 325

Everyman.
Gramercy, my friends and kinsmen kind!
Now shall I show you the grief of my mind.
I was commanded by a messenger

That is a High King's chief officer.   330
He bade me go a pilgrimage to my pain,
And I know well I shall never come again;
And I must give a reckoning strait,
For I have a great enemy that lieth for me in wait,
Who intendeth me to hinder.   335

Kindred.
What account is that which you must render?—
That would I know.

Everyman.
Of all my works I must show
How I have lived and my days have spent,
    Also of evil deeds to which I have been used   340
In my time, since life was to me lent,
    And of all virtues that I have refused.
Therefore, I pray you, go thither with me
To help to make my account, for Saint Charity!

Cousin.
What, to go thither? Is that the matter?   345
Nay, Everyman, I had liefer fast on bread and water
All this five year and more!

Everyman.
Alas, that ever my mother me bore!†
For now shall I never merry be,
If that you forsake me!   350

Kindred.
Ah, sir, come! Ye be a merry man!
    Pluck up heart and make no moan.
But one thing I warn you, by Saint Anne,
    As for me, ye shall go alone!

Everyman.
My cousin, will you not with me go?   355

Cousin.
No, by our Lady! I have the cramp in my toe.
Trust not to me, for, so God me speed,
I will deceive you in your utmost need.

Kindred.
It availeth not us to coax and court.†

Ye shall have my maid, with all my heart. 360
She loveth to go to feasts, there to make foolish sport
   And to dance, and in antics to take part.†
To help you on that journey I will give her leave willingly,
If so be that you and she may agree.

Everyman.
Now show me the very truth within your mind— 365
Will you go with me or abide behind?

Kindred.
Abide behind? Yea, that I will, if I may—
Therefore farewell till another day!

Everyman.
How shall I be merry or glad?—
   For fair promises men to me make, 370
   But, when I have most need, they me forsake!
I am deceived—that maketh me sad!

Cousin.
Cousin Everyman, farewell now, lo!
For, verily, I will not with thee go.
Also of mine own an unready reckoning, 375
I have to give account of, therefore I make tarrying.
Now God keep thee, for now I go!
               [*Kindred and Cousin go.*

Everyman.
Ah, Jesus, is all to this come so?
Lo, "fair words make fools fain,"
They promise, and from deeds refrain.† 380
My kinsmen promised me faithfully
For to abide by me stedfastly,
And now fast away do they flee.
Even so Fellowship promised me.
What friend were it best for me to provide?† 385
I am losing my time longer here to abide.
Yet still in my mind a thing there is,
All my life I have loved riches.
If that my Goods now help me might,
He would make my heart full light. 390
To him will I speak in my sorrow this day.
My Goods and Riches, where art thou, pray?
       [*Goods is disclosed hemmed in by chests and bags.*

Goods.
Who calleth me? Everyman? Why this haste thou hast?
> I lie here in corners trussed and piled so high,
And in chests I am locked so fast,   395
> Also sacked in bags, thou mayest see with thine eye,
I cannot stir; in packs, full low I lie.
What ye would have, lightly to me say.

Everyman.
Come hither, Goods, with all the haste thou may,
For counsel straightway I must ask of thee.   400

Goods.
Sir, if ye in this world have sorrow or adversity,
That can I help you to remedy shortly.

Everyman.
It is another disease that grieveth me;
In this world it is not, I tell thee so,
I am sent for another way to go,   405
To give a strict account general
Before the highest Jupiter† of all,
And all my life I have had joy and pleasure in thee,
Therefore I pray thee go with me,
For, peradventure, thou mayest before God Almighty on high   410
My reckoning help to clean and purify,
For one may hear ever and anon
That "money maketh all right that is wrong."

Goods.
Nay, Everyman, I sing another song—
I follow no man on such voyages,   415
For, if I went with thee,
Thou shouldest fare much the worse for me,
For, because on me thou didst set thy mind,
Thy reckoning I have made blotted and blind,
So that thine account thou canst not make truly—   420
And that hast thou for the love of me.

Everyman.
That would be to me grief full sore and sorrowing,†
When I should come that fearful answering.
Up, let us go thither together!

Goods.
Nay, not so! I am too brittle, I may not endure,   425
I will follow no man one foot, be ye sure.

Everyman.
Alas! I have thee loved, and had great pleasure
All the days of my life in goods and treasure.

Goods.
That is to thy damnation, I tell thee a true thing,
For love of me is to the love everlasting contrary.   430
But if thou hadst the while loved me moderately,
In such wise as to give the poor a part of me,
Then would'st thou not in this dolor be,
Nor in this great sorrow and care.

Everyman.
Lo, now was I deceived ere I was ware,   435
And all I may blame to misspending of time.

Goods.
What, thinkest thou I am thine?

Everyman.
I had thought so.

Goods.
Nay, Everyman, I say no.
Just for a while I was lent to thee,   440
A season thou hast had me in prosperity.
My nature it is man's soul to kill,
If I save one, a thousand I do spill.
Thinkest thou that I will follow thee?
Nay, from this world not, verily!   445

Everyman.
I had thought otherwise.

Goods.
   So it is to thy soul Goods is a thief,
For when thou art dead I straightway devise
Another to deceive in the same wise
   As I have done thee, and all to his soul's grief.   450

Everyman.
O false Goods, cursed may thou be!
Thou traitor to God that hast deceived me,
And caught me in thy snare.

Goods.
Marry, thou broughtest thyself to this care,—
Whereof I am glad!   455
I must needs laugh, I cannot be sad!

Everyman.
Ah, Goods, thou hast had long my hearty love.
I gave thee that which should be the Lord's above.
But wilt thou not go with me, indeed?—
    I pray thee truth to say!   460

Goods.
No, so God me speed!
    Therefore farewell, and have good-day.
                      [Goods is hidden from view.

Everyman.
Oh, to whom shall I make my moan
    For to go with me on that heavy journey!
First Fellowship, so he said, would have with me gone,   465
    His words were very pleasant and gay,
But afterwards he left me alone;
Then spake I to my kinsmen, all in despair,
And they also gave me words fair,
They lacked not fair speeches to spend,†   470
But all forsook me in the end;
Then went I to my Goods that I loved best,
In hope to have comfort, but there had I least,
For my Goods sharply did me tell
That he bringeth many into hell.   475
Then of myself I was ashamed,
And so I am worthy to be blamed.
Thus may I well myself hate.
Of whom shall I now counsel take?
I think that I shall never speed   480
Till I go to my Good Deeds.
But, alas! she is so weak,
That she can neither move nor speak.
Yet will I venture on her now.
My Good Deeds, where be you?   *[Good Deeds is shown.*   485

Good Deeds.
Here I lie, cold in the ground.
Thy sins surely have me bound
That I cannot stir.

Everyman.
O Good Deeds, I stand in fear!
I must pray you for counsel,   490
For help now would come right well!

Good Deeds.
Everyman, I have understanding
    That ye be summoned your account to make
Before Messias, of Jerusalem King.†
    If you do my counsel, that journey with you will I take.   495

Everyman.
    For that I come to you my moan to make.
I pray you that ye will go with me.

Good Deeds.
I would full fain, but I cannot stand, verily.

Everyman.
Why, is there something amiss that did you befall?

Good Deeds.
Yea, Sir, I may thank you for all.   500
If in every wise ye had encouraged me,
Your book of account full ready would be.
Behold the books of your works and your deeds thereby.
Ah, see, how under foot they lie
    Unto your soul's deep heaviness.   505

Everyman.
Our Lord Jesus his help vouchsafe to me,
For one letter here I cannot see.

Good Deeds.
    There is a blind reckoning in time of distress!

Everyman.
Good Deeds, I pray you help me in this need,
Or else I am forever damned indeed.   510
Therefore help me to make reckoning
Before him, that Redeemer is of everything,
That is, and was, and shall ever be, King of All.

Good Deeds.
Everyman, I am sorry for your fall,
And fain would I help you, if I were able.   515

Everyman.
Good Deeds, your counsel, I pray you, give me.

Good Deeds.
That will I do, verily.
Though on my feet I may not go,
I have a sister that shall with you be, also,
Called Knowledge, who shall with you abide,   520
  To help you to make that dire reckoning.
               [*Knowledge enters.*

Knowledge.
Everyman, I will go with thee and be thy guide,
In thy utmost need to go by thy side.

Everyman.
  In good condition I am now in every thing,
  And am wholly content with this good thing,   525
Thanks be to God, my creator!

Good Deeds.
And when he hath brought thee there,
  Where thou shalt heal thee of thy smart,
Then go with thy reckoning and thy good deeds together,
  For to make thee joyful at heart   530
Before the Holy Trinity.†

Everyman.
My Good Deeds, gramercy!
I am well content, certainly,
With your words sweet.

Knowledge.
Now go we together lovingly   535
To Confession, that cleansing river fair.

Everyman.
For joy I weep—I would we were there!
But, I pray you, give me cognition,
Where dwelleth that holy man, Confession?

Knowledge.
In the House of Salvation. 540
We shall find him in that place,
That shall us comfort by God's grace.

[Confession enters.
Lo, this is Confession. Kneel down, and ask mercy,
For he is in good favor with God Almighty.

Everyman.
O glorious fountain that all uncleanness doth clarify, 545
Wash from me the spots of vice unclean,
That on me no sin be seen!
I come with Knowledge for my redemption,
Redeemed with heartfelt and full contrition,
For I am commanded a pilgrimage to take, 550
And great accounts before God to make.
Now I pray you, Shrift, Mother of Salvation,
Help my good deeds because of my piteous exclamation!

Confession.
I know your sorrow well, Everyman,
    Because with Knowledge ye come to me. 555
I will you comfort as well as I can,
    And a precious stone will I give thee,
    Called penance, voice-voider of adversity.†
    Therewith shall your body chastened be
Through abstinence and perseverance in God's service. 560
Here shall you receive that scourge of me
That is penance stronge, that ye must endure,
To remember thy Saviour was scourged for thee
With sharp scourges, and suffered it patiently—
So must thou ere thou escape from that painful pilgrimage. 565
Knowledge, do thou sustain him on this voyage,
And by that time Good Deeds will be with thee.
But in any case be sure of mercy,
For your time draweth on fast, if ye will saved be.
Ask God mercy, and he will grant it truly. 570
When with the scourge of penance man doth him bind,
The oil of forgiveness then shall he find.

[Confession goes.

Everyman.
Thanked be God for his gracious work,
    For now will I my penance begin.
This hath rejoiced and lightened my heart, 575
    Though the knots be painful and hard within.

Knowledge.
Everyman, see that ye your penance fulfil,
    Whatever the pains ye abide full dear,[†]
And Knowledge shall give you counsel at will,
    How your account ye shall make full clear.   580

Everyman.
O eternal God, O heavenly being,
O way of righteousness, O goodly vision,
Which descended down into a virgin pure
Because he would for every man redeem
    That which Adam forfeited by his disobedience—
O blessed God, elect and exalted in thy divinity,   585
    Forgive thou my grievous offence!
    Here I cry thee mercy in this presence.

O spiritual treasure, O ransomer and redeemer,
Of all the world the hope and the governor,   590
Mirror of joy, founder of mercy,
Who illumineth heaven and earth thereby,
Hear my clamorous complaint, though late it be,
Receive my prayers, unworthy in this heavy life!
Though I be a sinner most abominable,   595
Yet let my name be written in Moses' table. [†]

O Mary,[†] pray to the Maker of everything
To vouchsafe me help at my ending,
And save me from the power of my enemy,
For Death assaileth me strongly!—   600
And, Lady, that I may, by means of thy prayer,
In your Son's glory as partner share,
Through the mediation of his passion I it crave.
I beseech you, help my soul to save!

Knowledge, give me the scourge of penance;   605
My flesh therewith shall give acquittance.
I will now begin, if God give me grace.

Knowledge.
Everyman, God give you time and space!
Thus I bequeath you into the hands of our Saviour,
Now may you make your reckoning sure.   610

Everyman.
In the name of the Holy Trinity,
My body sorely punished shall be.

Take this, body, for the sin of the flesh.
As thou delightest to go gay and fresh,
And in the way of damnation thou didst me bring,   615
Therefore suffer now the strokes of punishing.
Now of penance to wade the water clear I desire,
To save me from purgatory, that sharp fire.

Good Deeds.
I thank God now I can walk and go,
And am delivered of my sickness and woe!   620
Therefore with Everyman I will go and not spare;
His good works I will help him to declare.

Knowledge.
Now, Everyman, be merry and glad,
Your Good Deeds cometh now, ye may not be sad.
Now is your Good Deeds whole and sound,
Going upright upon the ground.   625
                        [*Good Deeds rises and walks to them.*

Everyman.
My heart is light and shall be evermore.
Now will I smite faster than I did before.

Good Deeds.
Everyman, pilgrim, my special friend,
Blessed be thou without end!   630
For thee is prepared the eternal glory.
Now thou hast made me whole and sound this tide,
In every hour I will by thee abide.

Everyman.
Welcome, my Good Deeds! Now I hear thy voice,
    I weep for sweetness of love.   635

Knowledge.
Be no more sad, but ever rejoice!
    God seeth thy manner of life on his throne above.
    Put on this garment to thy behoof,
Which wet with the tears of your weeping is,
Or else in God's presence you may it miss,   640
When ye to your journey's end come shall.

Everyman.
Gentle Knowledge, what do you it call?

Knowledge.
A garment of sorrow it is by name,
From pain it will you reclaim.
Contrition it is,   645
That getteth forgiveness,
Passing well it doth God please.

Good Deeds.
Everyman, will you wear it for your soul's ease?†

[*Everyman puts on the robe of contrition.*

Everyman.
Now blessed be Jesu, Mary's son,
For now have I on true contrition!   650
And let us go now without tarrying.
Good Deeds, have we all clear our reckoning?

Good Deeds.
Yea, indeed, I have them here.

Everyman.
Then I trust we need not fear.
Now, friends, let us not part in twain!   655

Knowledge.
Nay, Everyman, that will we not, for certain.

Good Deeds.
Yet must thou lead with thee
    Three persons of great might.

Everyman.
Who should they be?

Good Deeds.
    Discretion and Strength they hight.   660
And thy Beauty may not abide behind.

Knowledge.
Also ye must call to mind
Your Five Wits as your counsellors beside.

Good Deeds.
You must have them ready at every tide.

Everyman.
How shall I get them hither? 665

Knowledge.
You must call them all together,
And they will hear you immediately.

Everyman.
My friends, come hither and present be,
Discretion, Strength, my Five Wits, and Beauty.

[*They enter.*

Beauty.
Here at your will be we all ready. 670
What will ye that we should do?

Good Deeds.
That ye should with Everyman go,
And help him in his pilgrimage.
Advise you—will you with him or not, on that voyage?

Strength.
We will all bring him thither, 675
    To help him and comfort, believe ye me!

Discretion.
So will we go with him all together.

Everyman.
    Almighty God, beloved mayest thou be!
I give thee praise that I have hither brought
Strength, Discretion, Beauty, Five Wits—lack I nought— 680
And my Good Deeds, with Knowledge clear,
All be in my company at my will here.
I desire no more in this my anxiousness.

Strength.
And I, Strength, will stand by you in your distress,
Though thou wouldest in battle fight on the ground. 685

Five Wits.
And though it were through the world round,
We† will not leave you for sweet or sour.

Beauty.
No more will I unto Death's hour,
Whatsoever thereof befall.

Discretion.
Everyman, advise you first of all.   690
Go with a good advisement and deliberation.
We all give you virtuous monition
That all shall be well.

Everyman.
My friends, hearken what I will tell.
I pray God reward you in his heavenly sphere.   695
Now hearken all that be here,
For I will make my testament
Here before you all present.
    In alms, half my goods will I give with my hands twain,
In the way of charity with good intent,   700
    And the other half still shall remain
In bequest to return where it ought to be.
This I do in despite of the fiend of hell,
Out of his peril to quit me well
For ever after and this day.   705

Knowledge.
Everyman, hearken what I say.
Go to Priesthood, I you advise,
And receive of him in any wise
The Holy Sacrament† and Unction together,
Then see ye speedily turn again hither.   710
We will all await you here, verily.

Five Wits.
Yea, Everyman, haste thee that ye may ready be.
There is no emperor, king, duke, nor baron bold,
That from God such commission doth hold
As he doth to the least priest in this world consign,   715
For of the Blessed Sacraments, pure and benign,
He beareth the keys, and thereof hath the cure
For man's redemption, it is ever sure,
Which God as medicine for our souls' gain
Gave us out of his heart with great pain,   720
Here in this transitory life for thee and me.
Of the Blessed Sacraments seven there be,
Baptism, Confirmation, with Priesthood good,
And the Sacrament of God's precious Flesh and Blood,

Marriage, the Holy Extreme Unction, and Penance. 725
These seven are good to have in remembrance,
Gracious Sacraments of high divinity.

Everyman.
Fain would I receive that holy body.
And meekly to my spiritual father will I go.

Five Wits.
Everyman, that is best that ye can do. 730
God will you to salvation bring,
For Priesthood exceedeth every other thing.
To us Holy Scripture† they do teach,
And convert men from sin, heaven to reach.
God hath to them more power given 735
Than to any angel that is in heaven.
With five words he may consecrate
God's body in flesh and blood to make,
And handleth his Maker between his hands.
The priest bindeth and unbindeth all bands 740
Both in earth and heaven.—
Thou†dost administer all the Sacraments seven.
Though we should kiss thy feet, yet thereof thou worthy wert.
Thou art the surgeon that doth cure of mortal sin the hurt.
Remedy under God we find none 745
Except in Priesthood alone.—
Everyman, God gave priests that dignity,
And setteth them in his stead among us to be,
Thus be they above angels in degree.

Knowledge.
If priests be good, it is so surely; 750
But when Jesus hung on the cross with grievous smart,
There he gave out of his blessed heart
That same Sacrament in grievous torment.—
He sold them not to us, that Lord omnipotent.
Therefore Saint Peter the apostle† doth say 755
That Jesus' curse have all they
Which God their Saviour do buy or sell,
Or if they for any money do "take or tell."†
Sinful priests give sinners bad example in deed and word,
Their children sit by other men's fires, I have heard, 760
And some haunt of women the company,
With life unclean as through lustful acts of lechery—
These be with sin made blind.

Five Wits.
I trust to God no such may we find.
Therefore let us do Priesthood honor,   765
And follow their doctrines for our souls' succor.
We be their sheep, and they shepherds be,
By whom we all are kept in security.
Peace! for yonder I see Everyman come,
Who unto God hath made true satisfaction.   770

Good Deeds.
Methinketh it is he indeed.

Everyman.
Now may Jesus all of you comfort and speed!
I have received the Sacrament for my redemption,
And also mine extreme unction.
Blessed be all they that counselled me to take it!   775
And now, friends, let us go without longer respite.
I thank God ye would so long waiting stand.
Now set each of you on this rood your hand,
And shortly follow me.
I go before where I would be.   780
God be our guide!

Strength.
Everyman, we will not from you go,
    Till ye have gone this voyage long.

Discretion.
I, Discretion, will abide by you also.

Knowledge.
    And though of this pilgrimage the hardships be never so strong, 785
No turning backward in me shall you know.
Everyman, I will be as sure by thee,†
As ever I was by Judas Maccabee.†

Everyman.
Alas! I am so faint I may not stand,
    My limbs under me do fold.   790
Friends, let us not turn again to this land,
    Not for all the world's gold,
For into this cave must I creep,
And turn to the earth, and there sleep.

Beauty.
What—into this grave! Alas! Woe is me! 795

Everyman.
Yea, there shall ye consume utterly.

Beauty.
And what,—must I smother here?

Everyman.
Yea, by my faith, and never more appear!
In this world we shall live no more at all,
But in heaven before the highest lord of all. 800

Beauty.
I cross out all this! Adieu, by Saint John!†
I take "my tap in my lap"† and am gone.

Everyman.
What, Beauty!—whither go ye ?

Beauty.
Peace! I am deaf, I look not behind me,
Not if thou wouldest give me all the gold in thy chest. 805

[*Beauty goes, followed by the others, as they speak in turn.*

Everyman.
Alas! in whom may I trust!
Beauty fast away from me doth hie.
She promised with me to live and die.

Strength.
Everyman, I will thee also forsake and deny,
Thy game liketh me not at all! 810

Everyman.
Why, then ye will forsake me all!
Sweet Strength, tarry a little space.

Strength.
Nay, Sir, by the rood of grace,
I haste me fast my way from thee to take,
Though thou weep till thy heart do break. 815

Everyman.
Ye would ever abide by me, ye said.

Strength.
Yea, I have you far enough conveyed.
Ye be old enough, I understand,
Your pilgrimage to take in hand.
I repent me that I thither came.   820

Everyman.
Strength, for displeasing you I am to blame.
Will ye break "promise that is debt"?

Strength.
In faith, I care not!
Thou art but a fool to complain,
You spend your speech and waste your brain.   825
Go, thrust thyself into the ground!

Everyman.
I had thought more sure I should you have found,
But I see well, who trusteth in his Strength,
She him deceiveth at length.
Both Strength and Beauty have forsaken me,   830
Yet they promised me fair and lovingly.

Discretion.
Everyman, I will after Strength be gone—
As for me, I will leave you alone.

Everyman.
Why, Discretion, will ye forsake me!

Discretion.
Yea, in faith, I will go from thee,   835
For when Strength goeth before
I follow after, evermore.

Everyman.
Yet, I pray thee, for love of the Trinity
Look in my grave once in pity of me.

Discretion.
Nay, so nigh will I not come, trust me well!   840
Now I bid you each farewell.

Everyman.
Oh, all things fail save God alone—
Beauty, Strength, and Discretion!
For when Death bloweth his blast,
They all run from me full fast.   845

Five Wits.
Everyman, my leave now of thee I take.
I will follow the others, for here I thee forsake.

Everyman.
Alas! then may I wail and weep,
    For I took you for my best friend.

Five Wits.
I will thee no longer keep.   850
    Now farewell, and here's an end!

Everyman.
O Jesu, help! All have forsaken me.

Good Deeds.
Nay, Everyman, I will abide by thee,
    I will not forsake thee indeed!
    Thou wilt find me a good friend at need.   855

Everyman.
Gramercy, Good Deeds, now may I true friends see.
They have forsaken me everyone,
I loved them better than my Good Deeds alone.
Knowledge, will ye forsake me also?

Knowledge.
Yea, Everyman, when ye to death shall go,   860
But not yet, for no manner of danger.

Everyman.
Gramercy, Knowledge, with all my heart!

Knowledge.
Nay, yet will I not from hence depart,
Till whereunto ye shall come, I shall see and know.

Everyman.
Methinketh, alas! that I must now go   865
To make my reckoning, and my debts pay,

For I see my time is nigh spent away.
Take example, all ye that this do hear or see,
How they that I love best do forsake me,
Except my Good Deeds that abideth faithfully.   870

Good Deeds.
All earthly things are but vanity.
Beauty, Strength and Discretion do man forsake,
Foolish friends and kinsmen that fair spake,
All flee away save Good Deeds, and that am I!

Everyman.
Have mercy on me, God most mighty,   875
And stand by me, thou Mother and Maid, holy Mary!

Good Deeds.
Fear not, I will speak for thee.

Everyman.
Here I cry God mercy!

Good Deeds.
Shorten our end and minish our pain,
Let us go and never come again.   880

Everyman.
Into thy hands, Lord, my soul I commend—
    Receive it, Lord, that it be not lost!
As thou didst me buy, so do thou me defend,
    And save me from the fiend's boast
That I may appear with that blessed host   885
That shall be saved at the day of doom.
    In manus tuas,† of mights the most,
Forever *commendo spiritum meum.*†
                    [*Everyman goes into the grave.*

Knowledge.
Now that he hath suffered that we all shall endure,
The Good Deeds shall make all sure;   890
Now that he hath made ending,
Methinketh that I hear angels sing,
And make great joy and melody,
Where Everyman's soul shall received be!
                    [*The Angel appears.*

The Angel.

> Come, excellent elect spouse to Jesu!   895
>> Here above shalt thou go,
> Because of thy singular virtue.
>> Now thy soul from thy body is taken, lo!
> Thy reckoning is crystal clear.
> Now shalt thou into the heavenly sphere,   900
> Unto which ye all shall come
> That live well before the day of doom.
>> *[The Angel goes and the Doctor enters.*

Doctor.

> This moral men may have in mind,—
>> Ye hearers, take it as of worth, both young and old,
> And forsake Pride, for he deceiveth you in the end, as ye will find, 905
>> And remember Beauty, Five Wits, Strength, and Discretion,
>>> all told,
> They all at the last do Everyman forsake
> Save that his Good Deeds there doth he take.
> But beware, if they be small,
> Before God he hath no help at all,   910
> None excuse for Everyman may there then be there.
> Alas, how shall he then do and fare!
> For after death amends may no man make,
> For then Mercy and Pity do him forsake.
> If his reckoning be not clear when he doth come,   915
> God will say, *Ite, maledicti, in ignem aeternum.*†
> And he that hath his account whole and sound,
> High in heaven he shall be crowned,
> Unto which place God bring us all thither
> That we may live, body and soul, together!   920
> Thereto their aid vouchsafe the Trinity—
> Amen, say ye, for holy Charity!

FINIS.

*Thus endeth this moral play of **Everyman.***

The Second Shepherds' Play

Reading Pointers for Sharper Insights

The Second Shepherds' Play is, not surprisingly, the second play about shepherds in the Towneley/Wakefield Cycle. The first came immediately before this one, and many scholars believe the second play is actually a revision of the first. The Wakefield/Towneley Cycle is a series of thirty-two pageants based on the Bible, that was performed in the town of Wakefield, England, during the late Middle Ages and into the early Renaissance. It is also called the Towneley Cycle because the one existing manuscript that contains all thirty-two plays was once owned by the Towneley family.

It is entirely likely that, as a young boy, William Shakespeare was entertained by pageants such as *The Second Shepherds' Play*.

To better appreciate the impact of the play on its medieval audience, the reader should be aware of how and why these "cycle" or "mystery" plays were performed. In an era when there was virtually no local, daily entertainment—no organized sports, no local theater for live performances, no music except perhaps in church—the common person eagerly anticipated the springtime when, in the weeks following the festival of Easter, most towns and cities would host their pageant cycle. Caravans of colorful double-deckered wagons paraded the streets, and short plays dramatizing key stories from the Old and New Testaments would be performed on these wagons. The juxtaposition of past and present, contemporary and biblical, common and holy would surely move the medieval spectators in ways no formal sermon ever could. The excitement of the festival, the riotous colors of the wagons and costumes, and the noise of performers and crowd all combined to create an unforgettable experience for people whose lives were hard and for whom fun was scarce.

The thirty-two plays in the cycle were clearly written by several authors over the course of approximately two hundred years. However, several plays, including *The Second Shepherds' Play,* are so superior to the others that they are believed to have been authored by one playwright, today known simply as the Wakefield Master. Other plays in the cycle presumed to be by the Master include *Noah, The First Shepherds' Play, Herod the Great,* and *The Buffeting of Christ.* The assumed common authorship of these specific plays is based on their comedy, social satire, and sympathetic and realistic portrayal of humanity.

By watching the performances in this parade of plays, even a Middle Ages peasant could sample the full scope of biblical history, from Creation to Judgment. *The Second Shepherds' Play* is the Cycle's Nativity play, but the anonymous "Wakefield Master" tells this familiar tale with a comic twist that has made this one of the most famous medieval cycle plays still in existence.

Several of the plays are written in a unique pattern, sometimes called the "Wakefield Stanza." When reading, *The Second Shepherds' Play,* you might notice that the rhyme is both unusual and remains the same throughout the play. It is a nine-line stanza with the rhyme scheme AAAAB CCCB. In addition, each of the first four lines contains a caesura. The last word before the caesura in every line rhymes. For example, *The Second Shepherds' Play* begins:

> Lord, but this weather is *cold*, // and I am ill **wrapped**!
> Night dazed, were the truth *told*, // so long have I **napped**;
> My legs under me *fold*; // my fingers are **chapped**—
> With such like I don't *hold*, // for I am all **lapt**
> > In **sorrow**.
> s
> In storms and **tempest**,
> Now in the east, now in the **west**,
> Woe is him has never **rest**
> > Midday nor **morrow**!

Other plays in the Wakefield/Towneley Cycle include:
The Creation
The Slaying of Abel
The stories of *Abraham, Isaac, and Jacob*
The Exodus
The First Shepherds' Play
The Flight into Egypt
The Raising of Lazarus
The Crucifixion
The Parable of the Talents
The Resurrection
The Ascension
The Last Judgment

THE SECOND SHEPHERDS' PLAY

[*The First Shepherd (Primus Pastor) enters.*]

Primus Pastor.

    Lord, but this weather is cold, and I am ill wrapped!
    Night dazed, were the truth told, so long have I napped;
    My legs under me fold; my fingers are chapped—
    With such like I don't hold, for I am all lapt
            In sorrow.   5
    In storms and tempest,
    Now in the east, now in the west,
    Woe is him has never rest
            Midday nor morrow!

    But we seely shepherds that walk on the moor,   10
    In faith we're nigh at hand to be put out of door.
    No wonder, as it doth stand, if we be poor,
    For the tilth of our land lies fallow as the floor,
            As ye ken.
    We're so burdened and banned,   15
    Over-taxed and unmanned,
    We're made tame to the hand
            Of these gentry men.

Thus they rob us of our rest, our Lady them harry!
These men bound to their lords' behest,† they make the plough tarry, 20
What men say is for the best, we find the contrary,—
Thus are husbandmen oppressed, in point to miscarry,
    In life,
Thus hold they us under
And from comfort sunder.   25
It were great wonder,
     If ever we should thrive.

For if a man may get an embroidered sleeve or a brooch now-a-days,
Woe is him that may him grieve, or a word in answer says!
No blame may he receive, whatever pride he displays;   30
And yet may no man believe one word that he says,
    Not a letter.
His daily needs are gained
By boasts and bragging feigned,
And in all he's maintained   35
    By men that are greater.

Proud shall come a swain as a peacock may go,
He must borrow my wain, my plough also,
Then I am full fain to grant it ere he go.
Thus live we in pain, anger, and woe   40
    By night and day!
He must have it, if he choose,
Though I should it lose,
I were better hanged than refuse,
    Or once say him nay!   45

It does me good as I walk thus alone
Of this world for to talk and to make my moan.
To my sheep will I stalk, and hearken anon,
There wait on a balk, or sit on a stone.
    Full soon,   50
For I trow, pardie,
True men if they be,
We shall have company,
    Ere it be noon.

[*The First Shepherd goes out (or to one side).*
The Second Shepherd enters.]

Secundus Pastor.

Ben'cite and Dominus!† What may this mean?   55
Why fares the world thus! The like often we've seen!
Lord, but it is spiteful and grievous, this weather so keen!
And the frost so hideous—it waters mine een!
        That's no lie!
Now in dry, now in wet,   60
Now in snow, now in sleet,
When my shoes freeze to my feet,
        It's not all easy!

But so far as I ken, wherever I go,
We seely wedded men suffer mickle woe,   65
We have sorrow once and again, it befalls oft so.
Seely Capel, our hen, both to and fro
        She cackles,
But if she begins to croak,
To grumble or cluck,   70
Then woe be to our cock,
        For he is in the shackles!†

These men that are wed have not all their will;
When they're full hard bestead, they sigh mighty still;
God knows the life they are led is full hard and full ill,   75
Nor thereof in bower or bed may they speak their will,
        This tide.
My share I have found,
Know my lesson all round,
Woe is him that is bound,   80
        For he must it abide!

But now late in men's lives (such a marvel to me
That I think my heart rives such wonders to see,
How that destiny drives that it should so be!)
Some men will have two wives and some men three   85
        In store.
Some are grieved that have any,
But I'll wager my penny
Woe is him that has many,
        For he feels sore!   90

But young men as to wooing, for God's sake that you bought,
Beware well of wedding, and hold well in thought,
"Had I known" is a thing that serves you nought.
Much silent sorrowing has a wedding home brought,
           And grief gives,   95
With many a sharp shower—
For thou mayest catch in an hour
What shall taste thee full sour
           As long as one lives!

For—if ever read I epistle!—I have one by my fire,[†]   100
As sharp as a thistle, as rough as a briar,
She has brows like a bristle and a sour face by her;
If she had once wet her whistle, she might sing clearer and higher[†]
           Her pater-noster;[†]
She is as big as a whale,   105
She has a gallon of gall,—
By him that died for us all,[†]
           I wish I had run till I had lost her!

Primus Pastor.
    "God look over the row!" like a deaf man ye stand.

Secundus Pastor.
    Yea, sluggard, the devil thy maw burn with his brand!   110
    Didst see aught of Daw?

Primus Pastor.
                  Yea, on the pasture-land
    I heard him blow just before; he comes nigh at hand
           Below there.
    Stand still.

Secundus Pastor.
          Why?

Primus Pastor.
          For he comes, hope I.   115

Secundus Pastor.
    He'll catch us both with some lie
          Unless we beware.

[*The Third Shepherd enters, at first without seeing them.*]

Tertius Pastor.

 Christ's cross me speed and St. Nicholas!†
 Thereof in sooth I had need, it was worse than it was.
 Whoso hath knowledge, take heed, and let the world pass, 120
 You may never trust it, indeed,—it's as brittle as glass,
   As it rangeth.
 Never before fared this world so,
 With marvels that greater grow,
 Now in weal, now in woe, 125
   And everything changeth.

 There was never since Noah's flood such floods seen,
 Winds and rains so rude and storms so keen;
 Some stammered, some stood in doubt, as I ween.—
 Now God turn all to good, I say as I mean! 130
   For ponder
 How these floods all drown
 Both in fields and in town,
 And bear all down,
   And that is a wonder! 135

 We that walk of nights our cattle to keep,
   [*Catches sight of the others.*
 We see startling sights when other men sleep.
 Yet my heart grows more light—I see shrews a-peep.
 Ye are two tall wights—I will give my sheep
   A turn, below. 140
 But my mood is ill-sent;
 As I walk on this bent,
 I may lightly repent,
   If I stub my toe.
 Ah, Sir, God you save and my master sweet! 145
 A drink I crave, and somewhat to eat.

Primus Pastor.

 Christ's curse, my knave, thou'rt a lazy cheat!

Secundus Pastor.

 Lo, the boy lists to rave! Wait till later for meat,
   We have eat it.

Ill thrift on thy pate!   150
Though the rogue came late,
Yet is he in state
      To eat, could he get it.

Tertius Pastor.
That such servants as I, that sweat and swink,
Eat our bread full dry gives me reason to think.   155
Wet and weary we sigh while our masters wink,
Yet full late we come by our dinner and drink—
      But soon thereto
Our dame and sire,
When we've run in the mire,   160
Take a nip from our hire,
      And pay slow as they care to.

But hear my oath, master, since you find fault this way,
I shall do this hereafter—work to fit my pay;
I'll do just as much, sir, and now and then play,   165
For never yet supper in my stomach lay
      In the fields.
But why dispute so?
Off with staff I can go.
"Easy bargain," men say,   170
      "But a poor return yields."

Primus Pastor.
Thou wert an ill lad for work to ride wooing
From a man that had but little spending.

Secundus Pastor.
Peace, boy, I bade! No more jangling,
Or I'll make thee full sad, by the Heaven's King,   175
      With thy gauds!
Where are our sheep, boy? Left lorn?

Tertius Pastor.
Sir, this same day at morn,
I left them in the corn
      When they rang Lauds.   180

They have pasture good, they cannot go wrong.

Primus Pastor.

    That is right. By the Rood, these nights are long!

    Ere we go now, I would someone gave us a song.

Secundus Pastor.

    So I thought as I stood, to beguile us along.

Tertius Pastor.

             I agree. 185

Primus Pastor.

    The tenor I'll try.

Secundus Pastor.

    And I the treble so high.

Tertius Pastor.

    Then the mean shall be I.

             How ye chant now, let's see!

                [*They sing (the song is not given).*]

      Tunc entrat Mak, in clamide se super togam vestitus.[†]

Mak.

    Now, Lord, by thy seven names' spell,[†] that made both moon

        and stars on high, 190

    Full more than I can tell, by thy will for me, Lord, lack I.

    I am all at odds, nought goes well—that oft doth my temper try.

    Now would God I might in heaven dwell, for there no children cry,

          So still.

Primus Pastor.

    Who is that pipes so poor? 195

Mak.

    Would God ye knew what I endure!

[*Primus Pastor.*]

    Lo, a man that walks on the moor,

          And has not all his will!

Secundus Pastor.

    Mak, whither dost speed? What news do you bring?   200

Tertius Pastor.

    Is he come? Then take heed each one to this thing.

              Et accipit clamiden ab ipso.†

Mak.

    What! I am a yeoman—since there's need I should tell you—of the
        King,
    That self-same, indeed, messenger from a great lording,
              And the like thereby.
    Fie on you! Go hence
    Out of my presence!   205
    I must have reverence,
             And you as "who am I!"

Primus Pastor.

    Why dress ye it up so quaint? Mak, ye do ill!

Secundus Pastor.

    But, Mak, listen, ye saint, I believe what ye will!

Tertius Pastor.

    I trow the knave can feint, by the neck the devil him kill!   210

Mak.

    I shall make complaint, and you'll all get your fill,†
             At a word from me—
    And tell your doings, forsooth!

Primus Pastor.

    But, Mak, is that truth?
    Now take out that southern tooth   215
             And stick in a flea!

Secundus Pastor.

    Mak, the devil be in your eye, verily! to a blow I'd fain treat you.

Tertius Pastor.

    Mak, know you not me? By God, I could beat you!

Mak.

> God keep you all three! Me thought I had seen you—I greet you,
> Ye are a fair company!

Primus Pastor.

> Oh, now you remember, you cheat, you!   220

Secundus Pastor.

> Shrew, jokes are cheap!
> When thus late a man goes,
> What will folk suppose?—
> You've a bad name, God knows,
> For stealing of sheep!   225

Mak.

> And true as steel am I, all men know and say,
> But a sickness I feel, verily, that grips me hard, night and day.
> My belly is all awry, it is out of play—

Tertius Pastor.

> "Seldom doth the Devil lie dead by the way—"

Mak.

> Therefore   230
> Full sore am I and ill,
> Though I stand stone still;
> I've not eat a needle
> This month and more.

Primus Pastor.

> How fares thy wife, by my hood,† how fares she, ask I?   235

Mak.

> Lies asprawl, by the Rood, lo, the fire close by,
> And a house-full of home-brewed she drinks full nigh—
> Ill may speed any good thing that she will try
> Else to do!—
> Eats as fast as may be,   240
> And each year they'll a day be
> She brings forth a baby,
> And some years two.

But were I now kinder, d'ye hear, and far richer in purse,
Still were I eaten clear out of house and home, sirs.   245
And she's a foul-favored dear, see her close, by God's curse!
No one knows or may hear, I trow, of a worse,
           Not any!
Now will ye see what I proffer?—
To give all in my coffer,   250
To-morrow next to offer
           Her head-mass penny.†

Secundus Pastor.
    Faith, so weary and worn is there none in this shire.
    I must sleep, were I shorn of a part of my hire.

Tertius Pastor.
    I'm naked, cold, and forlorn, and would fain have a fire.   255

Primus Pastor.
    I'm clean spent,† for, since morn, I've run in the mire.
           Watch thou, do!

Secundus Pastor.
    Nay, I'll lie down hereby,
    For I must sleep, truly.

Tertius Pastor.
    As good a man's son was I,   260
           As any of you!
                [*They prepare to lie down.*
    But, Mak, come lie here in between, if you please.

Mak.
    You'll be hindered, I fear, from talking at ease,
           Indeed!
                [*He yields and lies down.*
    From my top to my toe,   265
    Manus tuas commendo,†
    Poncio Pilato,†
           Christ's cross me speed!
        Tunc surgit, pastoribus dormientibus, et dicit:†
Now 't were time a man knew, that lacks what he'd fain hold,
To steal privily through then into a fold,   270

And then nimbly his work do—and be not too bold,
For his bargain he'd rue, if it were told
   At the ending
Now 't were time their wrath to tell!—
But he needs good counsel   275
That fain would fare well,
    And has but little for spending.

But about you a circle as round as a moon,
           [*He draws the circle.*
Till I have done what I will, till that it be noon,
That ye lie stone still, until I have done;   280
And I shall say thereto still, a few good words soon
    Of might:
Over your heads my hand I lift.
Out go your eyes! Blind be your sight!
But I must make still better shift,   285
    If it's to be right.

Lord, how hard they sleep—that may ye all hear!
I never herded sheep, but I'll learn now, that's clear.
Though the flock be scared a heap, yet shall I slip near.
          [*He captures a sheep.*
Hey—hitherward creep! Now that betters our cheer   290
    From sorrow.
A fat sheep, I dare say!
A good fleece, swear I may!
When I can, then I'll pay,
    But this I will borrow!   295

[*Mak goes to his house, and knocks at the door.*]

Mak.
 Ho, Gill, art thou in? Get us a light!

Uxor Eius.[†]
 Who makes such a din at this time of night?
 I am set for to spin, I think not I might
 Rise a penny to win! Curses loud on them light
    Trouble cause!
              300
 A busy house-wife all day
 To be called thus away!

No work's done, I say,
>   Because of such small chores!

Mak.

The door open, good Gill. See'st thou not what I bring?   305

Uxor.

Draw the latch, an thou will. Ah, come in, my sweeting!

Mak.

Yea, thou need'st not care didst thou kill me with such long standing!

Uxor.

By the naked neck still thou art likely to swing.

Mak.

>   Oh, get away!
I am worthy of my meat,   310
For at a pinch I can get
More than they that swink and sweat
>   All the long day.

Thus it fell to my lot, Gill! Such luck came my way!

Uxor.

It were a foul blot to be hanged for it some day.   315

Mak.

I have often escaped, Gillot, as risky a play.

Uxor.

But "though long goes the pot to the water," men say,
>   "At last
Comes it home broken."

Mak.

Well know I the token,   320
But let it never be spoken—
>   But come and help fast!

I would he were slain, I would like well to eat,
This twelvemonth was I not so fain to have some sheep's meat.

Uxor.

    Should they come ere he's slain and hear the sheep bleat— 325

Mak.

    Then might I be a ta'en. That were a cold sweat!

              The door—

    Go close it!

Uxor.

              Yes, Mak,—

    For if they come at thy back— 330

Mak.

    Then might I suffer from the whole pack

             The devil, and more!

Uxor.

    A good trick have I spied, since thou thinkest of none,

    Here shall we him hide until they be gone—

    In my cradle he'll bide—just you let me alone—

    And I shall lie beside in childbed and groan. 335

Mak.

           Well said!

    And I shall say that this night

    A boy child saw the light.†

Uxor.

    Now that day was bright

           That saw me born and bred! 340

    This is a good device and a far cast.

    Ever a woman's advice gives help at the last!

    I care not who spies! Now go thou back fast!

Mak.

    Save I come ere they rise, there'll blow a cold blast!

        [Mak goes back to the moor, and prepares to lie down.]

           I will go sleep. 345

    Still sleeps all this company,

    And I shall slip in privily

    As it had never been I

           That carried off their sheep.

Primus Pastor.

 Resurrex a mortruis!† Reach me a hand!　　　　　　350
 Judas carnas dominus!† I can hardly stand!
 My foot's asleep, by Jesus, and my mouth's dry as sand.
 I thought we had laid us full night to England!

Secundus Pastor.

    Yea, verily!
 Lord, but I have slept well.　　　　　　355
 As fresh as an eel,
 As light do I feel,
    As leaf on the tree.

Tertius Pastor.

 Ben 'cite be herein! So my body is quaking,
 My heart is out of my skin with the to-do it's making.　　　　　　360
 Who's making all this din, so my head's set to aching.
 To the doer I'll win! Hark, you fellows, be waking!
    Four we were—
 See ye aught of Mak now?

Primus Pastor.

 We were up ere thou.　　　　　　365

Secundus Pastor.

 Man, to God I vow,
    Not once did he stir.

Tertius Pastor.

 Methought he was lapt in a wolf's skin.

Primus Pastor.

 So many are wrapped now—namely within.

Tertius Pastor.

 When we had long napped, methought with a gin　　　　　　370
 A fat sheep he trapped, but he made no din.

Secundus Pastor.

    Be still!
 Thy dream makes thee mad,
 It's a nightmare you've had.

Primus Pastor.

> God bring good out of bad, 375
> > If it be his will!

Secundus Pastor.

> Rise, Mak, for shame! Right long dost thou lie.

Mak.

> Now Christ's Holy Name be with us for aye!
> What's this, by Saint James,[†] I can't move when I try.
> I suppose I'm the same. Oo-o, my neck's lain awry 380
> > Enough, perdie—
> Many thanks![†]—since yester even.
> Now, by Saint Stephen,[†]
> I was plagued by a sweven,
> > Knocked at the heart of me. 385
>
> I thought Gill begun to croak and travail full sad,
> Well-nigh at the first cock,[†] with a young lad
> To add to our flock. Of that I am never glad,
> To have "tow on my rock more than ever I had."[†]
> > Oh, my head! 390
> A house full of young banes—
> The devil knock out their brains!
> Woe is him many gains,
> > And thereto little bread.
>
> I must go home, by your leave, to Gill, as I thought. 395
> Prithee look in my sleeve that I steal naught.
> I am loath you to grieve, or from you take aught.

Tertius Pastor.

> Go forth—ill may'st thou thrive!   [*Mak goes.*
> > Now I would that we sought
> > This morn, 400
> That we had all our store.

Primus Pastor.

> But I will go before.
> Let us meet.

Secundus Pastor.

>   Where, Daw?

Tertius Pastor.

>   At the crooked thorn.   405

>   [*They go out. Mak enters and knocks at his door.*]

Mak.

>   Undo the door, see who's here! How long must I stand?

Uxor Eius.

>   Who's making such gear? Now "walk in the wenyand."†

Mak.

>   Ah, Gill, what cheer? It is I, Mak, your husband.

Uxor.

>   Then may we "see here the devil in a band,"†

>   Sir Guile!   410

>   Lo, he comes with a note

>   As he were held by the throat.

>   And I cannot devote

>   To my work any while.

Mak.

>   Will ye hear the pother she makes to get her a gloze—   415

>   Naught but pleasure she takes, and curls up her toes.

Uxor.

>   Why, who runs, who wakes, who comes, who goes,

>   Who brews, who bakes, what makes me hoarse, d'ye suppose!

>   And also,

>   It is ruth to behold,   420

>   Now in hot, now in cold,

>   Full woeful is the household

>   That no woman doth know!

>   But what end hast thou made with the shepherds, Mak?

Mak.

>   The last word that they said when I turned my back   425

Was they'd see that they had of their sheep all the pack.
They'll not be pleased, I'm afraid, when they their sheep lack,
    Perdie.
But how so the game go,
They'll suspect me, whether or no,   430
And raise a great bellow,
    And cry out upon me.

But thou must use thy sleight.

Uxor.

     Yea, I think it not ill.
I shall swaddle him aright in my cradle with skill.   435
Were it yet a worse plight, yet a way I'd find still.

[*Gill meanwhile swaddles the sheep and places him in the cradle.*]

I will lie down forthright. Come tuck me up.

Mak.

    That I will.

Uxor.

   Behind!
    [*Mak tucks her in at the back.*
If Coll come and his marrow,   440
They will nip us full narrow.

Mak.

But I may cry out "Haro,"
    The sheep if they find.

Uxor.

Harken close till they call—they will come anon.
Come and make ready all, and sing thou alone—   445
Sing lullaby, thou shalt, for I must groan
And cry out by the wall on Mary and John†
    Full sore.†
Sing lullaby on fast,
When thou hear'st them at last,   450
And, save I play a shrewd cast,
    Trust me no more.

[*The Shepherds enter on the moor and meet.*]

Tertius Pastor.
　　Ah, Coll, good morn! Why sleepest thou not?

Primus Pastor.
　　Alas, that ever I was born! We have a foul blot.
　　A fat wether have we lorn.　　　　　　　　　　　　455

Tertius Pastor.
　　　　　　　　Marry, God forbid, say it not!

Secundus Pastor.
　　Who should do us that scorn? That were a foul spot.

Primus Pastor.
　　　　　　　Some shrew.
　　I have sought with my dogs
　　All Horbury Shrogs,†　　　　　　　　　　　　　　460
　　And of fifteen hogs
　　　　　　　　Found I all but one ewe.

Tertius Pastor.
　　Now trust me, if you will, by Saint Thomas of Kent,†
　　Either Mak or Gill their aid therto lent!

Primus Pastor.
　　Peace, man, be still! I saw when he went.　　　　465
　　Thou dost slander him ill. Thou shouldest repent
　　　　　　　　At once, indeed!

Secundus Pastor.
　　So may I thrive, perdie,
　　Should I die here where I be,
　　I would say it was he　　　　　　　　　　　　　　470
　　　　　　　　That did the same deed!

Tertius Pastor.
　　Go we thither, quick sped, and run on our feet,
　　I shall never eat bread till I know all complete!

Primus Pastor.

    Nor drink in my head till with him I meet.

Secundus Pastor.

    In no place will I bed until I him greet,   475
                 My brother!
    One vow I will plight,
    Till I see him in sight,
    I will ne'er sleep one night
                 Where I do another!   480

      [*They go to Mak's house. Mak, hearing them coming, begins
    to sing lullaby at the top of his voice, while Gill groans in concert.*]

Tertius Pastor.

    Hark the row they make! List our sire there croon!

Primus Pastor.

    Never heard I voice break so clear out of tune.
    Call to him.

Secundus Pastor.

              Mak, wake there! Undo your door soon!

Mak.

    Who is that spake as if it were noon?   485
               Aloft?
    Who is that, I say?

Tertius Pastor.

    Good fellows, if it were day—   [*Mocking* **Mak.**

Mak.

    As far as ye may,
               Kindly, speak soft;   490

    O'er a sick woman's head in such grievous throes!†
    I were liefer dead than she should suffer such woes.

Uxor.

    Go elsewhere, well sped. Oh, how my pain grows—
    Each footfall ye tread goes straight through my nose
               So loud, woe 's me!   495

Primus Pastor.

>   Tell us, Mak, if ye may,
>   How fare ye, I say?

Mak.

>   But are ye in this town to-day—
>   Now how fare ye?

>   Ye have run in the mire and are wet still a bit,   500
>   I will make you a fire, if ye will sit.
>   A nurse I would hire—can you help me in it?
>   Well quit is my hire—my dream the truth hit—
>   In season.
>   I have bairns, if ye knew,   505
>   Plenty more than will do,
>   But we must drink as we brew,
>   And that is but reason.

>   I would ye would eat ere ye go. Methinks that ye sweat.

Secundus Pastor.

>   Nay, no help could we know in what's drunken or eat.   510

Mak.

>   Why, sir, ails you aught but good, though?

Tertius Pastor.

>   Yea, our sheep that we get
>   Are stolen as they go; our loss is great.

Mak.

>   Sirs, Drink!
>   Had I been there,   515
>   Some one had bought it sore, I swear.

Primus Pastor.

>   Marry, some men trow what ye were,
>   And that makes us think!

Secundus Pastor.

>   Mak, one and another trows it should be ye.   520

Tertius Pastor.

> Either ye or your spouse, so say we.

Mak.

> Now if aught suspicion throws on Gill or me,
> Come and search our house, and then may ye see
> > Who had her—
> If I any sheep got, 525
> Or cow or stot;
> And Gill, my wife, rose not,
> > Here since we laid her.

> As I am true and leal, to God, here I pray
> That this is the first meal that I shall eat this day. 530

Primus Pastor.

> Mak, as may I have weal, advise thee, I say—
> "He learned timely to steal that could not say nay."

Uxor.

> > Me, my death you've dealt!
> Out, ye thieves, nor come again,
> Ye've come just to rob us, that's plain. 535

Mak.

> Hear ye not how she groans amain—
> > Your hearts should melt!

Uxor.

> From my child, thieves, begone. Go nigh him not,—there's the door!

Mak.

> If ye knew all she's borne, your hearts would be sore.
> Ye do wrong, I you warn, thus to come in before 540
> A woman that has borne—but I say no more.

Uxor.

> > Oh, my middle—I die!
> I vow to God so mild,
> If ever I you beguiled,
> That I will eat this child 545
> > That doth in this cradle lie!

Mak.

    Peace, woman, by God's pain, and cry not so.

    Thou dost hurt thy brain and fill me with woe.

Secundus Pastor.

    I trow our sheep is slain. What find ye two, though?

    Our work 's all in vain. We may as well go.   550

                 Save clothes and such matters

    I can find no flesh

    Hard or nesh,

    Salt nor fresh,

                 Except two empty platters.   555

    Of any "cattle"† but this, tame or wild, that we see,

    None, as may I have bliss, smelled as loud as he.

Uxor.

    No, so God joy and bliss of my child may give me!

Primus Pastor.

    We have aimed amiss; deceived, I trow, were we.

Secundus Pastor.

                 Sir, wholly each, one.   560

    Sir, Our Lady† him save!

    Is your child a knave?

Mak.

    Any lord might him have,

                 This child, for his son.

    When he wakes, so he grips, it's a pleasure to see.   565

Tertius Pastor.

    Good luck to his hips,† and blessing, say we!

    But who were his gossips, now tell who they be?

Mak.

    Blest be their lips—   [*Hesitates, at a loss.*

Primus Pastor

                 Hark a lie now, trust me!   [*Aside*

Mak.

              So may God them thank,   570
Parkin and Gibbon Waller, I say,
And gentle John Horn, in good fey—
He made all the fun and play—
              With the great shank.

Secundus Pastor.

    Mak, friends will we be, for we are at one.   575

Mak.

    We!—nay, count not on me, for amends get I none.
    Farewell, all three! Glad 't will be when ye're gone!
                    [*The Shepherds go.*

Tertius Pastor.

    "Fair words there may be, but love there is none
              This year."

Primus Pastor.

    Gave ye the child anything?   580

Secundus Pastor.

    I trow, not one farthing.

Tertius Pastor.

    Fast back I will fling.
              Await ye me here.

[*Daw goes back. The other Shepherds turn and follow
him slowly, entering while he is talking with **Mak**.*]

[*Tertius Pastor.*]

    Mak, I trust thou 'lt not grieve, if I go to thy child.

Mak.

    Nay, great hurt I receive,—thou has acted full wild.   585

Tertius Pastor.

    Thy bairn 't will not grieve, little day-star so mild.
    Mak, by your leave, let me give your child
             But six-pence.

[*Daw goes to the cradle, and starts to draw away the covering.*]

Mak.

    Nay, stop it—he sleeps!

Tertius Pastor.

    Methinks he peeps—   590

Mak.

    When he wakens, he weeps;
            I pray you go hence!
               [*The other Shepherds return.*

Tertius Pastor.

    Give me leave him to kiss, and lift up the clout.
    What the devil is this?—he has a long snout!

Primus Pastor.

    He's birth-marked amiss. We waste time hereabout.   595

Secundus Pastor.

    "A weft that ill-spun is comes ever foul out."
                   [*He sees the sheep.*
          Aye—so!
    He is like to our sheep!

Tertius Pastor.

    Ho, Gib, may I peep?

Primus Pastor.

    I trow "Nature will creep   600
            Where it may not go."

Secundus Pastor.

    This was a quaint gaud and a far cast.
    It was a high fraud.

Tertius Pastor.

    Yea, sirs, that was 't.
    Let's burn this bawd, and bind her fast.   605
    "A false scold," by the Lord, "will hang at the last!"
            So shalt thou!

Will ye see how they swaddle
His four feet in the middle!
Saw I never in the cradle 610
    A horned lad ere now!

Mak.

Peace, I say! Tell ye what, this to-do ye can spare!
                [*Pretending anger.*
It was I him begot and yon woman him bare.

Primus Pastor.

What the devil for name has he got? Mak?—
          Lo, God, Mak's heir! 615

Secundus Pastor.

Come, joke with him not. Now, may God give him care,
    I say!

Uxor.

A pretty child is he
As sits on a woman's knee,
A dilly-down, perdie, 620
    To make a man gay.

Tertius Pastor.

I know him by the ear-mark—that is a good token.

Mak.

I tell you, sirs, hark, his nose was broken—
Then there told me a clerk he'd been mis-spoken.

Primus Pastor.

Ye deal falsely and dark; I would fain be wroken. 625
    Get a weapon,—go!

Uxor.

He was taken by an elf,†
I saw it myself.
When the clock struck twelve,
    Was he mis-shapen so. 630

Secundus Pastor.

    Ye two are at one, that's plain, in all ye've done and said.

Primus Pastor.

    Since their theft they maintain, let us leave them dead!

Mak.

    If I trespass again, strike off my head!
    At your will I remain.

Tertius Pastor.

                  Sirs, take my counsel instead.   635
                  For this trespass
    We'll neither curse nor wrangle in spite,
    Chide nor fight,
    But have done forthright,
                  And toss him in canvas.   640

[They toss Mak in one of Gill's canvas sheets till they are tired. He disappears groaning into his house. The Shepherds pass over to the moor on the other side of the stage.]

Primus Pastor.

    Lord, lo! but I am sore, like to burst, in back and breast.
    In faith, I may no more, therefore will I rest.

Secundus Pastor.

    Like a sheep of seven score he weighted in my fist.
    To sleep anywhere, therefore seemeth now best.

Tertius Pastor.

                  Now I you pray,   645
    On this green let us lie.

Primus Pastor.

    O'er those thieves yet chafe I.

Tertius Pastor.

    Let your anger go by,—
                  Come do as I say.
                [As they are about to lie down the Angel appears.]
                Angelus cantat "Gloria in excelsis." Postea dicat:[†]

Angelus.

    Rise, herdsmen gentle, attend ye, for now is he born   650
    From that fiend that shall rend what Adam† had lorn,
    That warlock to shend, this night is he born,
    God is made your friend now on this morn.
                Lo! thus doth he command—
    Go to Bethlehem, see   655
    Where he lieth so free,
    In a manger full lowly
                'Twix where twain beasts stand.
                        [*The Angel goes.*

Primus Pastor.

    This was a fine voice, even as ever I heard.
    It is a marvel, by St. Stephen, thus with dread to be stirred.   660

Secundus Pastor.

    'T was of God's Son† from heaven he these tidings averred.
    All the wood with a levin, methought at his word
                Shone fair.

Tertius Pastor.

    Of a Child did he tell,
    In Bethlehem,† mark ye well.   665

Primus Pastor.

    That this star yonder doth spell—
                Let us seek him there.

Secundus Pastor.

    Say, what was his song—how it went, did ye hear?
    Three breves to a long—

Tertius Pastor.

    Marry, yes, to my ear   670
    There was no crotchet wrong, naught it lacked and full clear!

Primus Pastor.

    To sing it here, us among, as he nicked it, full near.
            I know how—

Secundus Pastor.

    Let's see how you croon!

    Can you bark at the moon?   675

Tertius Pastor.

    Hold your tongues, have done!

          Hark after me now!   [*They sing.*

Secundus Pastor.

    To Bethlehem he bade that we should go.

    I am sore adrad that we tarry too slow.

Tertius Pastor.

    Be merry, and not sad—our song's of mirth not of woe,   680

    To be forever glad as our meed may we know,

          Without noise.

Primus Pastor.

    Hie we thither, then, speedily,

    Though we be wet and weary,

    To that Child† and that Lady!—   685

          We must not lose those joys!

Secundus Pastor.

    We find by the prophecy—let be your din!—

    David† and Isaiah,† and more that I mind me therein,

    They prophesied by clergy, that in a virgin,

    Should he alight and lie, to assuage our sin,   690

          And slake it,

    Our nature, from woe,

    For it was Isaiah said so,

    "*Ecce virgo*

          Concipiet"† a child that is naked.   695

Tertius Pastor.

    Full glad may we be and await that day

    That lovesome one to see, that all mights doth sway.

    Lord, well it were with me, now and for aye,

    Might I kneel on my knee some word for to say

          To that child.   700

    But the angel said

    In a crib was he laid,

He was poorly arrayed,
>Both gracious and mild.

Primus Pastor.

>Patriarchs that have been and prophets beforne,   705
>They desired to have seen this child that is born.
>They are gone full clean,—that have they lorn.
>We shall see him, I ween, ere it be morn,
>>For token.
>When I see him and feel,   710
>I shall know full well,
>It is true as steel,
>>What prophets have spoken,

>To so poor as we are that he would appear,
>First find and declare by his messenger.   715

Secundus Pastor.

>Go we now, let us fare, the place is us near.

Tertius Pastor.

>I am ready and eager to be there; let us together with cheer
>>To that bright one go.
>Lord, if thy will it be,[†]
>Untaught are we all three,   720
>Some kind of joy grant us, that we
>>Thy creatures, comfort may know!

>[*They enter the stable and adore the infant Saviour.*]

Primus Pastor.

>Hail, thou comely and clean one! Hail, young Child!
>Hail, Maker, as I mean, from a maiden so mild!
>Thou hast harried, I ween, the warlock so wild,—   725
>The false beguiler with his teen now goes beguiled.
>>Lo, he merries,
>Lo, he laughs, my sweeting!
>A happy meeting!
>Here's my promised greeting,—   730
>>Have a bob of cherries!

Secundus Pastor.

    Hail, sovereign Saviour, for thou hast us sought!

    Hail, noble nursling and flower, that all things hast wrought!

    Hail, thou, full of gracious power, that made all from nought!

    Hail, I kneel and I cower! A bird have I brought   735

                To my bairn from far.

    Hail, little tiny mop!

    Of our creed thou art the crop,

    I fain would drink in thy cup,

                Little day-star!   740

Tertius Pastor.

    Hail, darling dear one, full of Godhead† indeed!

    I pray thee be near, when I have need.

    Hail, sweet is thy cheer! My heart would bleed

    To see thee sit here in so poor a weed,

                With no pennies.   745

    Hail, put forth thy dall,

    I bring thee but a ball,

    Keep it, and play with it withal,

                And go to the tennis.

Maria.

    The Father of Heaven this night, God omnipotent,   750

    That setteth all things alright, his Son hath he sent.

    My name he named and did light on me ere that he went.

    I conceived him forthright through his might as he meant,

                And now he is born.

    May he keep you from woe!   755

    I shall pray him do so.

    Tell it, forth as ye go,

                And remember this morn.

Primus Pastor.

    Farewell, Lady, so fair to behold

    With thy child on thy knee!   760

Secundus Pastor.

                But he lies full cold!

    Lord, 't is well with me! Now we go, behold!

Tertius Pastor.

    Forsooth, already it seems to be told
              Full oft!

Primus Pastor.

    What grace we have found!   765

Secundus Pastor.

    Now are we won safe and sound.

Tertius Pastor.

    Come forth, to sing are we bound.
              Make it ring then aloft.

                    [*They depart singing.*

           Explicit pagina Pastorum.†

Glossary
for
Everyman

the seven deadly sins – These are the seven characteristics identified in Christianity as sinful: Lust/Lechery (excessive sexual desire), Gluttony (overindulgence in alcohol or food), Greed (obsession with wealth or material things), Sloth (laziness), Wrath (violent anger), Envy/Covetousness (wanting what another has), Pride (vanity, too high opinion of oneself).

in briefest space – in all haste

passions to be   – tempests; temptations

thou shalt make none for thee attorney – Death will not negotiate on his behalf.

prince, or peer – During that time, a Duke was sometimes referred to as a prince.

Adam's sin – This refers to Adam and Eve. They ate the forbidden fruit from the tree of knowledge and were banished from Eden (paradise) as punishment for giving in to temptation.

Saint Charity – "Holy Charity"; compared to Saint Cross, Saint Sepulchre; Everyman is asking Death to show him charity.

vale terrestrial – mortal life on earth

wits five – the five senses: memory, imagination, estimation, fantasy, and common sense

would be – had been

by this day! – a medieval exclamation

gramercy – The word is from the from the French expression, *grant merci*. It literally means "great thanks," or "thanks exceedingly."

Adonai – a Hebrew name for God as an indication of respect

Pardy – This is derived from the French exclamation, "pardi," which is a contraction of the words *par Dieu*. The literal translation is "by God."

"Nature will creep where it may not go." – This proverb is used to assert the force of "nature," which enables it to produce effects from causes, even in cases where obstacles, apparently insuperable, are in the way. The meaning here is that blood relationship will force Everyman's kin to aid him in his distress, even though they want to refuse him.

Cousin – The word is used here as a general, as well as specific, title of relationship. Cousin, could mean a relative, friend, or acquaintance.

Alas, that ever my mother me bore! – Everyman exclaims that he regrets being born.

to coax and court – to entice

in antics to take part – to break loose from ordinary restrictions and have a good time.

and from deeds refrain – and will do nothing, indeed

for me to provide – to provide myself with

Jupiter – a reference to the Roman god of the heavens (used here as another name for God)

full sore and sorrowing – That would cause him much pain and sorrow.

"They lacked not fair speeches to spend." – "They spoke well."

Messias, of Jerusalem King – Jesus, the expected savior of the Jews

Holy Trinity – In Christianity, it is the belief that God is one being consisting of three people: the Father, Son, and Holy Spirit.

voice-voider of adversity – Confession gives Everyman a penance, which he must recite aloud. The penance will "void" Everyman's sins and purify him.

Whatever the pains ye abide full dear – Whatever pain it may be to you.

Moses' table – Moses led the Hebrew slaves out of Egypt after convincing the Pharaoh to free them. He performed many miracles, through God, including parting the Red Sea. He was given two stone tablets onto which God had inscribed the Ten Commandments.

Mary – In Christianity, she is known as the Virgin Mary, the mother of Jesus.

soul's ease – health

We – Five Wits uses the plural as representing the five senses, not as speaking for the others.

Holy Sacrament – This refers to the seven rites (in Catholicism) that were instituted by Jesus to confer grace: baptism, communion, penance, confirmation, matrimony, holy orders, and extreme unction.

Holy Scripture – the sacred writings of the Bible

Thou – Five Wits here apostrophizes Priesthood.

Saint Peter the apostle – In the Bible, an apostle was someone chosen by Jesus to preach his Gospel. Of the twelve apostles, Peter was one of the most prominent. He was also the first Bishop of Rome.

"take or tell" – a proverbial phrase expressing acts done unlawfully, as for a bribe

I will be as sure by thee – I will never part from you.

Judas Maccabee – Judah Maccabee, the Jewish patriot of the second century B.C.

Saint John – One of the apostles, he is said to have written the fourth Gospel and other passages in the Bible.

I take "my tap in my lap" and am gone. – The phrase is a proverbial expression, still or until recently used in parts of Scotland; "to take one's tap in one's lap and set off," literally refers to a housewife's gathering up her tap, the suitable quantity of flax for spinning, with her rock or distaff in her lap or apron to run in to, or go from, a friend's house, and hence proverbially to describe a hasty departure.

In manus tuas – [Latin] "Into thy hands"

commendo spiritum meum – [Latin] "I commend my spirit"

Ite, maledicti, in ignem aeternum – [Latin] "Depart, ye cursed, into everlasting fire"

Vocabulary
for
Everyman

abide – to continue for a long time

abstinence – the self-denial of something, especially alcohol, unhealthy food, or sexual relations

acquaintance – a person one knows, but not very well

acquittance – the release of a debt or obligation

adversity – a state of hardship or misfortune

Alack! – an exclamation of regret or sorrow

alms – money or goods given to the poor

begot – fathered; produced

behoof – an advantage, benefit

benign – gentle, not harmful

bequeath – to pass on to another

blind – hard to understand

caitiff – a detestable and cowardly person

celestial – relating to heaven

chastened – punished

clamorous – very loud or insistent

cognition – the act of knowing

commendable – worthy of approval or praise

commission – to charge with a task

consecrate – to make holy

consign – to entrust or assign

consume – to decay

contrition – sincere remorse for wrongdoing or sin

covetous – *[covet]* to want what another has

damnation – eternal punishment for sin

deliberation – careful thought before actions or decisions

discretion – the ability to make choices for oneself

doctrines – the teachings of a specific subject

dolor – grief, sorrow

dread – detest

ere – before

fain – eagerly, willingly

fellowship – a friendly relationship, companionship

forbear – to hold back, resist

forfeited – lost or gave up as a penalty

forsake – to abandon or give up on
grief – shame or disgrace
grievous – sorrowful or dreadful
hie – to hurry
hight – are named or called
knots – the effects of punishment
lechery – excessive desires of a sexual nature
liefer – readily or willingly
lightly – quickly
mediation – the process of resolving differences through an impartial person
minish – to lessen
mirth – fun, laughter
monition – *[admonition]* cautionary advice, a warning
nigh – near
nought – *[naught]* nothing
omnipotent – all powerful, having unlimited authority
penance – the punishment that follows confession of sin
peradventure – possibly
perseverance – steadily keeping to a course of action
pilgrimage – a long journey, usually holy in nature
piteously – sorrowfully; worthy of compassion
prithee – I pray thee; a polite request
proffered – offered
prosperity – having good fortune, especially concerning wealth
purgatory – a place of punishment; in Catholicism, a place where souls endure punishment for sin until they are purified by making amends
quick – alive
reckoning – an accounting of something
redeemer – one who relieves another of a debt (here referring to Jesus)
respite – a temporary delay of punishment for something unpleasant
reverence – an attitude of respect
righteousness – the quality of being morally upright
reposed – dependent upon
rood – the cross Everyman carries; a reference to the cross Jesus carried
salvation – being saved from the power and penalty of sin
scourge – a means of punishment
shrift – confession, followed by penance and absolution of sin
smite – to affect suddenly and strongly
solace – comfort during distress or sorrow
stedfastly – *[steadfastly]* adhering firmly in direction or purpose
strait – strict

succor – help, assistance
sustain – to support
tarrying – delaying, putting off
testament – a formal pledge to give something
transitory – lasting a short time, temporary
trussed – tied or bound tightly
Tush! – an exclamation of mild disapproval
twain – two
unction – the application of ointment in a religious ceremony
verily – truthfully; confidently
virtues – the principles of moral goodness
vouchsafing – granting or giving
wrath – extreme anger

Glossary
for
The Second Shepherds' Play

bound to their lords' behest – bound to nobles, referring, as the context seems to show, not to people in a servile condition, but to the nobles' agents employed to enforce their claims upon their tenants

Ben'cite and Dominus! – Ben'cite is a shortened form of *benedicite* (Latin for "bless you!"); Dominus means "God." These are frequent in medieval use, both as a salutation and exclamation.

"Seely Capel…in the shackles!" – The Shepherds are making an off-color joke about married men. The reference to shackles is a parallel to the modern phrase "ball and chain," which refers to the confines of marriage.

by my fire – "for my mate"

she might sing clearer and higher – "full and clear"; the phrase is probably proverbial, used in an ironic reference to a hoarse, rough voice.

pater-noster – Latin for *Our Father*, the first two words of the Lord's Prayer; it should be noted that the author isn't concerned about the accuracy of doctrine or dogma until the Angel arrives, which is almost at the end of the play. The author is more concerned with using crude jokes, ill humor, and curses for comedic effect with a festive audience.

By him that died for us all – a reference to Jesus Christ

St. Nicholas – a reference to Nicholas of Myra (died 345 AD); this Saint became known as Santa Claus.

Tunc entrat Mak, in clamide se super togam vestitus – [Latin] "Then enters Mak, who has put on a cloak above his ordinary dress."

seven names' spell – There are seven names for God in Hebrew: El, Elohim, Adonai, YHWH (Jahveh), Ehyer-Aher-Ehyeh, Shaddai, and Lebaot. The "spell" in the comment does not refer to a magical spell; instead it indicates that the names of God may not be spelled out.

Et accipit clamiden ab ipso – [Latin] "And takes the cloak off him."

you'll all get your fill – They will all suffer.

by my hood – an oath

"To give all…head-mass penny." – "If I could but pay for her burial mass."

clean spent – exhausted

Manus tuas commendo – [Latin] part of the phrase "I commend [my spirit] into your hands."

Poncio Pilato – [Latin] Pontius Pilate; according to the Bible, he ordered Jesus' crucifixion.

Tunc surgit, pastoribus dormientibus, et dicit: – [Latin] "Then he rises, when the shepherds are asleep, and says:"

Uxor Eius – [Latin] "his wife"

saw the light – was born

Resurrex a mortruis! – [Latin] "Resurrected from the dead!"

Judas carnas dominus! – [Latin] "Judas, lord in the flesh!"; this is a phrase expressing surprise and is similar to "Mary, mother of God." According to the Bible, Judas, a disciple, betrayed Jesus for forty pieces of silver.

Saint James – Known as St. James the Greater, he was one of Jesus' first disciples.

Many thanks! – either ironic to express his gratitude for his neck, or possibly in return for an attempt on the part of one of the shepherds to straighten it out for him

Saint Stephen – the first martyr of Christianity

first cock – daybreak; this refers to the first call of a rooster in the morning.

"tow on my rock more than ever I had" – literally, "more tow on my distaff to spin than ever before"; *tow* refers to flax or hemp that would be spun into yarn. The idiom means "more to look out for."

"walk in the wenyand" – "walk in the waning [moon]" i.e., "go where bad luck may find you"

"see here the devil in a band" – "There's the devil in the bond" i.e., "There's trouble in this arrangement." This phrase might mean, "the devil to pay."

Mary and John – Mary is Jesus' mother; John is probably John the Baptist.

full sore – loudly, fully

Horbury Shrogs – i.e., Horbury thickets—*shrogs* denotes rough land covered with thickets. Harbury is a town near Wakefield, with which the Towneley cycle is identified.

Saint Thomas of Kent – a disciple of Jesus; according to the Bible, after Jesus was crucified, He rose on the third day. He soon visited his disciples, and when Thomas heard about Jesus' resurrection, he said, "Unless I see the mark of the nails in his hands and put my finger into the nail marks and put my hand into his side, I will not believe." (John 20:25) He is known, therefore, as "Doubting Thomas."

in such grievous throes! – in great distress

"cattle" – a pun on "cattle" and "chattel"; chattel means personal property or slaves.

Our Lady – the Virgin Mary

"Good luck to his hips…" – "a fortunate future and happiness be to him in body" ; *hips* indicates the whole body. The phrase is a forced one to provide a rime for *gossips,* but its artificiality would not have seemed so great to a medieval hearer, owing to the practice of constantly referring to various parts of the body in blessing and cursing. Moreover, reference to the hip in a generic sense was frequently used, as in the phrases, "on the hip," "on his hip," and "on my hips," to denote a bad plight.

He was taken by an elf – Gill tries to pretend that an elf has substituted a sheep for the true child; it was believed that elves exchanged other creatures for babies to use the children as slaves.

Angelus cantat "Gloria in excelsis." Postea dicat: – [Latin] "The Angel sings 'Gloria in Excelsis.' Then let him say:"

Adam – According to the book of Genesis in the Bible, Adam was the first human that God created.

God's Son – another reference to Jesus

Bethlehem – where Jesus was born

Child – a reference to Jesus

David – the second king of Israel

Isaiah – a prophet and author of the biblical book that bears his name

"Ecce virgo Concipiet" – [Latin] "Behold, the virgin will conceive." This is a biblical passage that can be found in Isaiah 7:14.

Lord, if thy will it be – This paraphrases Jesus's words in the Garden of Gethsamene before He is crucified: "Thy will be done."

Godhead – a reference to the Trinity: Father, Son, and Holy Spirit

Explicit pagina Pastorum. – [Latin] "Here endeth the play of the Shepherds."

Vocabulary
for
The Second Shepherds' Play

adrad – frightened, filled with dread
alight – to come down and settle upon
amain – violently; with force
amends – compensation, payment
anon – soon
assuage – to alleviate or reduce
aught – anything; at all
averred – declared
awry – sour
bade – commanded
bairns – children
balk – a ridge or hillock
banes – irritations; things that cause constant annoyance
bawd – a prostitute
beforne – before
begot – fathered; produced
beguile – to distract or amuse pleasantly
bent – an unenclosed pasture; heath
bestead – used
bide – to be left
blot – a stain on one's character or reputation
bower – a woman's bedroom
brooch – a decorative pin
capel – a humorous name for a hen
chafe – to irritate
chide – to scold or express disapproval
clout – a cloth
cock – a synonym for rooster
coffer – a box used for holding valuables
cower – to hide or cringe in fear
creed – a formal statement of religious belief
croon – to sing in a soothing manner
crop – the head; top part
crotchet – a musical note
dall – a fist
day-star – the morning star (the planet Venus)

dilly-down – a darling

din – noise

een – eyes

epistle – a letter in the New Testament of the Bible

ewe – a full-grown female sheep

fallowed – plowed, but not seeded land

far cast – a clever trick

farthing – a coin worth one-quarter of a penny

feigned – deceived or pretended

feint – to deceive

fey – faith

fie – an interjection that is used to show displeasure

forsooth – in truth; indeed

free – nobly

gall – anger; bile

gauds – shrewd tricks, jokes

gay – happy

gin – a trap for catching animals

gloze – an excuse

gossips – sponsors

Haro – an expression meaning "Woe is me!" or "Help!"

harry – to disturb or harass

hence – away, at a distance

hie – to hurry

hogs – young sheep

home-brewed – home-made beer or liquor

jangling – making irritating noises

ken – to see or understand

knave – someone who is deceitful

Lauds – the first of the religious hours of daily service

leal – faithful, loyal, true

levin – lightning

liefer – readily or willingly

lorn – lost, forsaken, abandoned

marrow – company

maw – the mouth, usually of a ravenous creature

meed – a gift

mickle – great

mire – a bog

mirth – fun; laughter

mis-spoken – bewitched

moor – an area of open land that has course grasses and bogs

mop – literally, "fool"; used, however, as a term of endearment

nesh – susceptible to cold weather

nigh – near

nimbly – in a quick, easy manner

omnipotent – all-powerful; having unlimited authority

pardie [also *perdie*] – an oath meaning surely or truly

pate – the head

pence – a penny

pipes – sings

pother – to worry, trouble, or fuss

proffer – to offer

quaint – unfamiliar; strange

rives – rips, splits, or tears

Rood – a crucifix symbolizing the cross used in the Crucifixion

rue – to regret

ruth –sorrowful

scorn – an evil trick

seely – blameless and to be pitied; "poor"

shackles – in a tight place; under restraints

shank – a long leg

shend – to spoil; overthrow

shire – land

shrews – rascals

shrogs – thickets

slake – to take away

sleight – cleverness; trickery

sooth – truth; reality

sore – very, quite

speed – aid, protection

spied – created; thought of

spin – to make thread or yarn

spite – ill will

stot – a young bull

swain – a young shepherd

sweven – a dream

swink – to toil, labor

tarry – to delay; put off

tempest – a violent storm

tidings – news

tilth – the condition of soil

travail – labor; pain of childbirth

trow – to suppose

verily – truthfully; confidently

wain – a horse-drawn cart or carriage used in farming

wakes – watches

weal – prosperity and happiness

weed – a dress; covering

ween – to think

weft – a woven fabric

wights – humans; creatures

wink – to sleep

wrangle – to argue or bicker

wroken – revenged

yeoman – an attendant or servant